Lost and Found by the Muddy Banks

Poems by Sean Arnold

Kansas City Spartan Press Missouri

Spartan Press
Kansas City, Missouri
spartanpresskc.com

Spartan Press

Copyright (c) Sean Arnold, 2018
First Edition 1 3 5 7 9 10 8 6 4 2
ISBN: 978-1-946642-55-4
LCCN: 2018944950

Design, edits and layout: Jason Ryberg, Jason Braun
Cover image and author photo: Virginia Harold
All rights reserved. No part of this publication may be reproduced or transmitted in any form or by any means, electronic or mechanical, including photocopying, recording or by info retrieval system, without prior written permission from the author.

Spartan Press would like to thank Prospero's Books, The Fellowship of N-finite Jest, The Prospero Institute of Disquieted P/o/e/t/i/c/s, Will Leathem, Tom Wayne, Jeanette Powers, j d tulloch, Jon Bidwell, Jason Preu, Mark McClane, Tony Hayden and the whole Osage Arts Community.

The author would like to thank the following publications where some of these poems first appeared:

"St. Lucipher" first appeared in *Crossing the Divide.*
"St. Louis on Fire" first appeared in *Bad Jacket #7.*

CONTENTS

Big Jim Plays Shady Grove / 1

Soliloquy From a Freight Yard / 3

For Hemingway / 5

Cool Glass of Water / 6

Mercy and Pain, Pain of Mercy / 7

Love Poem / 8

St. Lucipher / 9

Social Services Worker / 11

Purgatory Forest Gump / 12

The Blessed Community / 13

The Waitress / 15

Progress Note —Treatment Plan for
  Mental Wellness / 17

The Dishwasher, Walking Home Late / 19

The Bear Man / 20

Abbey Ale / 22

The Carousel Motel / 24

First World Post Industrial
  Undergraduate Blues / 25

The Soliloquy of Fox Mulder / 27

That Creeping Shade of Death / 28

Shady Tree / 29

Coffee Drinkin' / 30

Honeymoon / 32

Maplewood / 36

Short Poems / 37

Running Shorts / 40

Las Vegas Gunman / 41

Oregon's on Fire / 42

Live Rust / 43

Running Poem / 44

One More Time with Feeling / 45

Holiday Record Snow / 46

Big Jim's Lone Satellite / 48

Big Jim's Commute / 51

Big Jim Dreams Lost Dream of the Belle
  Missouri Bookstore / 52

Big Jim Gets His Wisdom Teeth Yanked / 53

New Year / 54

Ode to The Wasteland / 55

St. Louis On Fire / 57

This book is dedicated to Jason Braun, Rooster Jake,
Nick Kuntz and Michelle Arnold.

Big Jim Plays Shady Grove

I would never tell Jim that washing dishes at the
   restaurant is nasty work—
Jim who stands on roofs and welds the steel siding plates
   for HVAC units.
Jim taking his 8-week work trip to South Dakota during
   the country's record cold front.
The company he works for, he says, makes too much
   profit but will only work him two days a week,
   so he's behind on electric, behind on gas, and behind
   on the mortgage for the wood-paneled house by the
   Mississippi where from the front porch he can see the
   river and the smelting plants' smoking siloes.
He's got the five kids, the wife, the new baby, the two
   puppies fighting raccoons and cats from the
   Carondelet alleys.
This would be a good bit of work, he says,
the heartache of necessity though too
leaving the family,
stranded in a rural no-man's land where the locals sell
   meat for twice the usual price because you're from
   out of town.
And there's no guessing what the HVAC journeyman of
   South Dakota are like;
   he tells me of his last time travelling for work on the
   Arkansas-Louisiana border in Texarkana —

The two men who got in a knife fight on the roof and were
    allowed to come back the next day,
him and his coworker standing 150 feet up on scaffolding
    in the simmering 115-degree heat wave welding a silo
and Jim looks down at the brown ponds below and says to
    his coworker *Shit, Red! I don't think those are fish
    down there. One of 'em just took a bite of something!
    Those are fucking alligators!*

He tunes his mandolin while telling me all this, telling me
    what I'm describing to you
    and starts playing *Shady Grove*
really wailing away at that mandolin held in his 6 foot
    4 inch 300 pound welder's hands.
Ya gotta do what ya gotta, he says,
The cold front should let up,
South Dakota will be a little warmer in a couple weeks.
Shady Grove, my darling.

Soliloquy From a Freight Yard

I would ride the rails
taking a running jump,
attaching myself to that huge and slow moving train
   like a barnacle.
I would jump off a couple miles down the line
and walk back to the dorms,
scuffed up from rolling onto the gravel.
Sometimes I would paint graffiti while I rode in those
   boxcars;
I felt the world pushing
and my mind filled with trepidation,
I thought that if I could free myself from college
the terror in my head would clear.
I yearned for life *somewhere else.*

I sought a true Big Rock Candy Mountains of the soul.
The rails could woosh me to a new kind of American
   lonely
in the huge sky and deserted industry of Montana
or famous weird California
or to the eerie rain and pine of Washington
or across the border to chilly springtime in Canadian
   forests.
Or I could have starved to death like Chris McCandless
stuck at the end of the line without a guide or a prayer
in wide-open Alaska.
I could have shuddered in crossroads of rail-lines and
   never found my way back.

But I stayed in St. Louis,
fading into the tuck pointed mortar of brick
in a decaying but alive part of town,
squatting houses and evading arrest,
confused in the mind
but finding contentment as it came.

For Hemingway

Memories of past soldiers and munitions,
past dog fights, barracudas, couldn't prepare for this;
a hurricane attacks the Florida coast
folds the violent winds inwards on Key West.
No argument or shotgun blasts at the sky could
dissuade its path. Still
your ghost fires a pistol
into the storm and a
word of pause from the prose of scientific fact.

Aftermath settles,
Hemmingway's lone bungalow lies
low in the rain still
in tact,
soaked, but alive approaches
a six toed cat.

Cool Glass of Water

Deprivation of the senses can seem so poetic
raw hallucinations
drug induced stupor
feeling starved.
But cold potato salad
a glass of ice water and
a fan on full blast
on a steaming hot day
are even better.

Loving you, Kelly is
like that. Before I met you
I was John the Baptist
crunching bitter locusts in the wilderness
not to say you are my Christ
taking me down to the river,
but the salvation is real enough.

Before I met you I frowned over
the sparse anxiety of being and
the loss of mind and my lonely.
Now, life is a bounty
real and comforting as your blue eyes.

What I'm saying is that you reveal things to me
you are the cool glass of water on
the balmy summer afternoon of my lifetime.

Mercy and Pain, Pain of Mercy

I think of the pain you've caused
the psychic pain of loss
the sexual pain
the pain of the body's ugly organs.

There is a muttering man
crumpled on his couch
unable to face the day
unable to face himself
unable to face us, his victims
his children, his paranoia, his
mistress.

That nasty cold I've been fighting all week
my wisdom teeth pushing through the gums
   of the old teeth.
Physician heal thyself
metphysician heal thyself.
I think of the mercy of my body fighting the cold virus.
Saving enough cash to get the teeth yanked
   and sawed out
living in a city that takes me to the bridge's edge
but won't let me walk over.

I babysit my father and his delusions so
my mom can sit in church
I think of all the mercy
all the mercy on this earth.

Love Poem

I don't really remember
the computers of my past
nor the shitty sedans
my parents bought me that all later broke down.
The cheap whiskey I've drunk in dusty rooms
the coffee in the afternoon, tea in paper cups
the old loves and crushes fade too
I think only
Of your sweet kiss.

St. Lucipher

I drive down highway 44 on my route home
plains and subtle hills across the Mississippi
graffiti in yellow outline and straight white letters
red brick duplexes
smell of iron drifts through my open fall car window
past Broadway trucker throws a butt out the window
sparks skidding across the breakdown lane.
I make it to my exit
got off near the Italian district turn onto Shaw
where last night the neighborhood's rental cop shot
that young black man to death.
My wife swears she heard the shots
twelve shots ringing into the darkness.
They say the dude pulled something out of his pocket
  before he died,
was it a gun, was it a sandwich?
Later that night more protests
real revolt springs up
from an unquiet pain
the world and city wait and watch my neighborhood
while cops brutalize in the streets and civilians
  push back.
Starting with a vigil then marching
shouts for justice, smashed cop car windows.
Some are saying the city's got a riot in its head.

Folks no longer willing to become accustomed
to this custom.
Another black man is deceased
Who's to blame — the police.
Sirens pulse in the background
the march turns scarce.

St. Louis, America
you long-suffering bastard.

Social Services Worker

Arms swollen from bed bugs, dry
and itching, comes onto the porch in
her nightie, stating I heard
where they give you $75, $100 for
Christmas, I haven't heard of that I
say, she goes upstairs, the guy who told her this,
affable, only one day of stubble
leather-faced, high cheekbones,
track marks and bug bites along his arms
he tells me *She always comin up with*
Information that later gets disproven,
Let's see if she can find that document about
The Christmas money.

In my line of work folks are always wondering
where the hookup is.
Like manna from heaven
we deliver social service information
try to help for the holidays.

Purgatory Forest Gump

The lightning in the night
chills out into a sedate cloud cover
a narrative of black coffee sitting in a floral mug
pretentious, artisanal,
gives way to the muscularity of milk.

I had a vision last night I was a teenager running down
   a dirt road in Kansas over and over
a purgatory Forrest Gump, running across the
dirt country
crossing the nation in the 1960s
crossing a Kansas county
crossing my imagination.
Then I wake, the day unfolded a sedate burning,
cloud cover, a delicate cooling mist
my quadriceps of creamer and still
I remember running.

The Blessed Community

The others could not touch us
we were the blessed community.

We were among the invasive vines
that grew along the brick of our squatted houses.
The buildings were falling down, we patched up the cracks
    and fixed up the walls
installed woodstoves
gathered wood the ministers around the way would give us
we shit in buckets and used the waste for compost
we protested and then hunkered down looking
for a cure for a civilization we saw as decedent.
We dug our nails into the fresh dirt, planting squash,
    mint and sweet potatoes.
Winter's barren ground will bring spring's fresh harvest,
    we said.

But I would walk to that old liquor store from my squat
get the cheapest tall boys I could muster the change for
two bottles of Mad Dog wine and a pack of Swishers,
walk back to the block and sit by my woodstove alone
    write my way through.
All those folks quarantined off from the world
I reassured myself that they had faith
in deliverance and rapture
they'd say damn this place to hell
the end is near.

I would slowly emerge
biking to the populated areas
sitting at the night coffee with a hot cup watching
   the people
growing belief in something else
that there was a world outside of us worth saving.

The Waitress

From the kitchen, steak-burgers hiss on the grill,
Neil Young guitar squall spills through front-of-the-
   house-speakers,
the espresso machine clangs,
steam rises from the steaming wand,
the waitress deftly handles the latte.
She floats across the wood floor,
balancing full glasses of water on the tray
so wonderfully secure in her hands.
Can I take your order? What'll that be tonight?
We have beef-tip melt and mushroom bisque,
and for dessert We have homemade cheesecake,
   gooey butter cake, and more!
Out the window a man with a light blue business shirt
   talks to a woman
   with a Steel Reserve in a brown paper bag.
The waitress's dimpled smile floats through the busy
   dinner atmosphere
I nurse a nearly empty beer as folks rub their goatees at
   a distant table
put on my pea coat and head toward the door,
   shuffling into the night.

Love, I am an onlooker here and
a surprise visitor

keeping you company at the café.
You come home at 4:30 am
where we finally sleep side by side
on a mattress made for royalty
till I rise in the morning
to wash the dishes
at a different café.

Progress Note —Treatment Plan for Mental Wellness

Service Date: 3/15/15

Time From: 1:20

Time To: 1:55

Organization: Metaphysic Counseling Service

Client: S----------------

Service Provided: Counseled client about talking to a character named "Thomas Waits." Client complained that the hallucination (of a visual and auditory nature) descended him into a hell of men with scrambled egg eyes and chimney ear canals. There was no way out, and this was an unartful hell. No amount of positive visualization could change that. Still, counseled client about combatting negative thought processes regarding him seeing "Mr. Waits." Counseled client to tell the negative thoughts to "Tom" in order to realize the unreality of the hallucination. Client's Schizophrenia was seemingly in remission; however this new development is troubling. Client missing one tooth, which he says is sore and rotting, although he doesn't remember how he lost it. Told client to have a nice birthday, and he seemed more at ease upon me finishing the visit.

Response From the Person Served: Waits drags me into a back alley hell, where even the gutsiest people won't go. The eyes of the beast are on me when I see Waits. Only Maury Povitch and Jesus can help me out. Jesus Christ is the pope on acid, and no counselor can convince me otherwise. I haven't been outside in months.

Yet my counselor sees my troubles. He has even seen figures like Waits in the past, he says. His counsel is sometimes wishy-washy yet a comfort in stormy seas. Jeez this is hard, but thanks to him I see a bit of hope. I'd like to get back to washing dishes at the Waffle House or something like that. Times were good then. I think that maybe things could change.

The Dishwasher, Walking Home Late
After Ikkyu

You'll find me in the dark
of February's smog,
crouched beneath the trees,
taking a piss into the moonlight.
Then I walk home crookedly through the alley,
breath acrid with gin,
the juices of the restaurant soaked into my shirt.
The bar stays open after the restaurant closes
so, I don't take my leave of that place till 3:30 in
  the morning
tired but with a smile,
admiring the city moon.

The Bear Man

For Timothy Treadwell

Those pool parties,
early girlfriends and gloomy parents.
Into the pool I jumped —
the slick sheen of water
where I could pretend I was a dolphin
or an orca whale
diving my way into college.
But I grew bitterness toward the college life,
so, I went west and never really came back.
Those beaches and the wannabe stars,
I tried to fit in,
almost got that starring role.
But they took it away
and I was left alone.
So I drifted onto the beach
where I would drink and swim,
and search for sharks and manta-rays.
There was a heart that took me to
Alaska.
Setting foot at the edge of a great expanse
I took my first great breath and saw them,
the beasts
with gentle paws,
elegant teeth,
perfect fur,
their graceful gait.

I was one of them.
I made a home with them in the wilderness.
I lived a curious life with the bears.
I would do speaking tours
get in front of the human cameras
wanting to free my fellow men
from the sickness
that was the human world.
In the bears I saw something that'd always escaped me,
though you wouldn't know by my pink flesh
and beach blonde hair,
I was one of them.

I thought I'd live forever
but would accept the brutality of fate if need be.

The salmon were scarcer that year,
the bears became agitated.
This surly one looked so tough
I would try to get closer
and end up feeling fear, not belonging.
I saw the brush being shaken and he wanted me
as he approached so tense and mean
I knew this was it.
In those gaping jaws I fought him.
I recorded my last movie
before I made that big and painful leap
into the dark rainbow of becoming
inside the bear-skin.

Abbey Ale

When asked the question, 'Do you enjoy your work'? Keeley throws his head back and erupts in jolly laughter, managing a few words between chuckles. 'I do, I do. I hope it's obvious.
—From a Brew Your Own Magazine interview with
Father Isaac Keeley, beer brewing Trappist monk.

We wake at 5:45
before the sun shines its nose through the stained-glass
   windows of the abbey.
We go to the dining hall,
eat our preserves on rye bread,

our souls made new with the waking.

Then we get to work in the brewing room
there are tanks taller and wider than several men.
This facility is state-of-the-art
but to me everything is so elegantly simple
as I take up my morning station
and start the bottles along the conveyer.

To thine be the glory

just like a Trappist meditation
chanting
in the silence of the abbey.

Some would say it's sinful to indulge,
but it's really just one beer for dinner on Sundays
the golden ale with the strong hop presence
6.5% alcohol, just right.
As for the work, you'd think
we'd profit like kings
but we limit our production so it's all
by the work of our hands.
God is still alive in the 21st century I would say

Forever and ever, thine kingdom come

alive and well in the brewing tank.

The Carousel Motel

Walking through the heat of North St. Louis
resisting the temptation to venture into Red's Liquor
  and Carry,
wild thoughts taunting me:
You don't deserve to live
and *Fuck them, their mothers are motherfuckers,*
and *Jesus Christ is a methadone pope.*
Keep going though, through the thin lawns and
  abandoned buildings of the North Side and
I make it to the Carousel Motel at last
check in with my bag full of all my stuff.
Through the thin walls
I hear arguing over a deal
I hear the children playing in the courtyard
jumping rope and threatening schoolyard enemies
Miss Mary Mac Mac Mac all dressed in black.
Telephone wires string up the clouds through the slit
  of open window
Jesus Christ is your almighty enemy, come home to me
  a voice says.
I take an anti-psychotic from a manila envelope labeled
  Tuesday,
the motel walls comforting as night fades and the sky
  rumbles.
As good a day as any to take refuge, I tell myself —
turn on Divorce Court
tired in my bones
drifting to sleep
on this mattress.

First World Post Industrial Undergraduate Blues

The darkness of the student loan
service industry job;
need, need, need; the computer, the car, the smartphone,
set to installments before your parents finally cut you off.
May there be no collapse of health, nor temporary insanity
as you stumble around looking for insurance.

She keeps the submissions coming, pays the submission fees up front,
works three different nanny gigs, screaming toddlers and earnest affections.
He buses the tables and is thinking about a second job because his MacBook needs repairs,
sets his poems to music on weekends in bars soaked with decay
cheap beer, cigarettes and a handful of friends.

You beg them for water
they give you gasoline.

But I once heard of folks who moved into abandoned houses
fixed them up, propped up the walls, installed woodstoves, composted,

grew vegetables and the like,
they paid no rent, lived days in ultimate leisure,
hunting squirrels from city trees and gathering berries
   from bushes.
I have heard that they were happy,
their story is a rumor on a hot, brutal and dusty wind,
And somewhere those same actual people
are fretting about the rising costs of caulk,
how hard it's getting to do the Home Depot scam,
and the difficulty in finding a decent part time
   dishwashing gig.

Somewhere the wolves are howling
in an unfettered wilderness,
I know, for I have been there.

First world problems, as they say.

The Soliloquy of Fox Mulder

The truth is out there in every Max Fennig,
schizophrenic UFO nuts with no hope but an airstream
 trailer
and an eye to the sky.
The poetry of the abduction,
the blinding spectacle,
the subtle beauty of mystery,
a whodunit where the stakes are humanity.
I would wander the lands looking for a trace,
a paper trail written in alien blood.
Shaggy monsters disappearing into the deep,
grainy film and a man who wanted to keep me from
 seeing it
Marlboro smoke curling up from an unknown office.
Hope; above all, I had hope.
Then they crushed it,
left me bewildered time and time again crying
to be re-employed.
I got what I wanted, and you can watch the premier
 15 years after the fact,
the second coming of
the X-Files.

That Creeping Shade of Death

When I shot the B.B. gun
my buddy Nick was holding my hand steady
in the backyards of Wichita, Kansas.
There was a dry heat those days,
and we would go down passages
behind the subdivisions to find
those dry tall-grass blades and elusive sparrows.
We'd shoot at cans, action figures and Barbie dolls.
This kid would later give me my first toke of weed
as we blared Hendrix in his dad's Mercedes coup.

One day he came to me with a wry look and said,
*Yesterday I shot a bluebird. Its wings flapped onto the
 ground then he was gone.*
That creeping shade of death
moving so slightly in Wichita's suburbs.
I got a queasy thrill from hearing about that bluebird,
a sacrifice to boyish curiosity
flapping crazily in the dirt,
maybe a last squawk,
a dying trophy in a dusty backyard,
something to ponder
while I wandered through the Best Buy outlets
  and Burger King courtyards.

Shady Tree

I'd like to be
beneath a shady tree
smoking cloves with my honey
sunshine and a crisp breeze
a book of Ikkyu and homemade mead.
We hear sirens in the distance
we pay them no mind.

Coffee Drinkin'

I started drinking coffee when I'd gone insane my first
  year of college;
wanting something to cut through the fog of madness,
  the tired terror of psychosis.
I was heavy, dog-tired from anti-psychotics and needed
  5-6 cups just to get my equilibrium back.
After the worst of the nightmare
I'd enjoy coffee's solace, alone, woeful yet proud to be
  reading poetry again in a coffeehouse, unemployed,
  hungry,
maybe some writer's cliché with a bad beatnik beard
  and a too-grumbling stomach
but the spike of caffeine illuminating my otherwise
  sluggish consciousness.
The coffeeshop was a place I could go and be alone
with other people;
the slick business hipsters on their laptops
the old lesbians peering over their cups
the other poets so solemn.
I'd eventually recover from the insanity,
the place let me be a part time barista,
making those lattes, the huge buzz of the espresso
  machine, the steaming wand whooshing in my hands.
Real work,
just above minimum wage never felt so good.

The bitter gas station road coffee
or the gourmet pour-over
I respect it all;
high voltage double brewed
on a beautiful balmy afternoon
window open,
the fog rolling through.
A jolt and a guide for a mind troubled but ready
to perceive the world.

Honeymoon

1. The flight;
windowless tunnel, pure
light, catch a flight
tired above the sky
landing, sheer excitement.

2. The drive from Belize City airport, through the countryside, to the resort

auto parts piled high
are we close to the jungle?
Scrubby bushes and palm trees,
big rivers
smoke, burning vegetation through the trees.
Incomprehensible green and gray shacks
dot the burned landscape
lush jagged mountains in the distance
definitely a foreigner here.

3. Waking up in the jungle
humid smoke of dew trees big as dinosaurs
green jungle
morning orchid garden.

4. Honeymoon
a cup of coffee
for you
my little hummingbird

5. What made you choose Belize?
her idea
she never
steers me wrong

6. Luxury, all inclusive
still no Wi-Fi
but lager included
we don't speak their language
but they speak ours
the barman shows me
his Mexican hip-hop sad clown tattoos.
Why clowns? Because life is freaky.

7. The cave
shining darkening pearl stalagmites
shining against a headlamp
stumbling through the darkness
to find a river
to find a rushing rapid waterfall deep in the cave
climb up it, 40 feet high,
plunge off, water rushing, cave jock poetry.

8. Time off social work

we ease into the days (remind
ourselves to relax)
days long as a cobweb to a fly.

9. Babe
breasts against the linens
she reads
the Ursula LeGuin book
she got as a wedding gift.

10. Shuttle to the beach
ride through the
highlands to the
swampy lowland peninsula

11. A beach of one's own
two chairs and an extra
stout, the sun so close white
heat, waves lapping against the white
beach, swirling clouds,
iguanas scuttle with horned mantles
waves on my toes sand on my toes
dig deeper till I find the tan sand.
A beach of one's own
a beach of the mind, no,
a reality beach.

12. Monsoon rains

plunge us into the relief of a cool night.

13) Away
from the heat of the city
we have only the heat
of the sun.

14) Flies buzz
around my ankles
in paradise.

15) The shuttle to leave
picks us up at 6am
we'll be back in St. Louis by
11pm, luggage scuttles finally
across sand.

16) Honeymoon ending
but everyday I'll
say I love you.

Maplewood

Sitting under the same
maplewood tree
for 10 years and writing my life.
A delectable
the wind on fire
crickets, cranes, telephone wires.
I see the moments accumulate
like sandbags at the foot of the busted levy.

Short Poems

My morning's rage
betrayed by
a kiss.

Addicted to two things:
caffeine,
folk Music.

Fall is alive
radiant crispness, bright reds, tans, spreading
through the neighborhood.

The taste of
lemon-water left out
overnight.

The space-lite eyes
of a person on a locked ward
of a psychiatric institution.

All day long we pass along
information, all day long we
pass along information all day
long.

The cat passes along the table
searching for
a coffee to knock over.

Folks with schizophrenia
are superheroes
creeping under the bridges of night.

Cat bites my leg
Satori means
kick-in-the-head.

Gray skies
cicadas chirp life.

Short poems
old neighbors
sharp whiskey.

Bike ride through another
bevo-mill cemetery
attacked by the gnats of South City.

Outdoor cat
big old eyes
curious and free.

Big first soup with
all the vegetables fresh from the garden
that the anarchists helped you cook.

Sly easy wind
lazy Sunday
lone ride home.

Another scorcher
then a cool day
silos groan in the distance.

Running Shorts

Poetry and long-distance running
exercises in wondrous futility.

He sees his striding shadow
besides himself in a public park
the darkening head
against a blazing sunrise.

Angry sweat and
a graceful stride
the poetry of the love of
repetition.

Waking at 5am
to run through
the cold sleeping neighborhood.

Used to run from cops
now I run from my old record times.

Freedom in the fall
a brisk tempo run
finishing like a
Pink Lady plucked from a tree.

Las Vegas Gunman

*Land
of a death without eyes*
-Lorca

No way to prevent this, says only nation where this regularly happens.
-The Onion

Moral intensity of an assault rifle ban (or denial thereof), too much psychology (don't blame mental illness), a vision of psyche (no known cause), twisting roulette table (blood on the black-jack dealers and country musicians), money wired to Vietnam (no ambiguity in politics or death), I read the news (what morning routine could break the crippling anxiety of being human), In Rome folks axed each other to death under the lion's gaze (perhaps we've always been rotten), maybe nature will finally take care of us (fresh start for the earth). No end in sight. The same commentary reprinted.

Oregon's on Fire

Oregon's on fire the waterfalled idea of beauty where
we walked along the gravel of a space-ship ledge, the
dark fall-off of the cliff, the hot mist. So many water
falls. Sticky clothes, Tim the guide, forest-fire-fighter
as a job, sure of himself. Ally Kelly and I faithfully
behind. The glow of sunlight. The dash to find the
campground before its populated. Creek beer, put a
beer from the backpack into the icy creek. I found a
secret place there, crisp white-foamed roaring rapids.
The rhythm of the river and I meditated there. Bonfire
in the cold night. We turned back ten miles the
next day, tired and clowning, tiny among pines.
Now I'm in Missouri, Tim fights the fire on the job,
he says he's seen it, he's fought it, where we were hiking
is scorched and changed forever. I see them over
beers in the winter. Sure enough it's gone, our spot
was scorched. We will never see it the same.

Live Rust

Tonight's the Night
I drink beer alone
satisfied/self-satisfied
not lonely merely alone
but still feeling like a creep in the
lowlight, a wheat ale in hand I write in my living-room
in my *man-chair* by
lamplight, amusing myself like a cat with a mouse
Neil Young on the turntable
telling me about a love
that never rusts or a love
that rusts too fast.
Like Rock N Roll thrown
to the dogs of punk rock
like Neil still kicking in his late 70s
after all he's seen,
the poets of his generation dying like flies
I feel only a twinge of knee-ache and laugh at the thought
  of 29 being old
or being existential because I've experienced
some set amount of heartache and nu-metal nostalgia
for lost gods of rock n roll I'll never know
things I'm likely too young to truly comprehend
like the Midwestern lightning and frost out the window
they'll never see or care for on the coasts.
This street less violent than others I've been on
this street with its rusted heart.

Running Poem

Back this fall when I was skinny
I was slimming constantly
and on fire for the answer
running 8-20 miles a day
running at dawn
through a muggy and tree-blanketed park
running at sunset, after the day job
one beer after
then a book
or making love
a vinyl record carrying me to an early sound sleep.

The blazing trees of fall begat an injury
big enough to stop me but small enough
that someday I'll recover. With it
a weariness, a meanness, two beers a night
whiskey. Love lost.

Slowly I am starting
over,
inching up the miles finding an innocent stride
it's winter and dark after work
I run in the chill
under streetlights gauzy with dust and low light,
get those miles in
3,4,6
but more miles to go till before I rest.

One More Time with Feeling

One more time with heart,
with the old saxophone of my heart
the vibrating tenor of mixed emotion, of
joy within joy itself and all the hate of the world at large.
Looking into the long night
finding a prophecy of you a while back
wishing for tender arms
nape of neck to kiss
to run a small index finger across
a prophecy of fluttering nimble lips
of the warm bath of your sex,
reaching towards me a dream
asleep in a purple velvet bed
a dream of you of your
big feckless love.
Of hard work and relief.
Your innate desire for all things big and small,
swirling red blonde curl,
the illustrated characters of your pearl blue eyes.
I wake, run the water over my shoulders
put in my balm, my mouthwash, my black coffee
your longing before I enter
the void of another day.

Holiday Record Snow

A true white Christmas
snow packed tight to the ground
clean, white, a touch of gray.
Old relatives spill, stumble out
onto the avenues
TV, the golden years of Charlie Brown
on the big screen, and
the genius of snowflakes.
A sort of hard-won, post-truth sadness, an anxiety
   of wars on Christmas
millennial fatigue, distrust, of baby-boomers and shitty
   adultery
worms its way into my Christmas brain as I worry about
   my mom.
An eerie flu, a pitiful cough plagues me. But
I have firm-packed stovetop espresso shooting steam
out of its tiny tin spigot and
reading a book that alt-Facebook could never
   comprehend; *The Snow Leopard.*
In which Peter Matthiessen a hound dog for Zen truth
seeing Milerapa's insane unity and clarity of all being
   in the present
over the leering white precipice of the 19,000-foot-
   and-climbing
Himalayas, his Sherpas

his selfish expedition partner
their journey is to look for the snow leopard
a yeti of a cat that they might never know.
Peter looks down off the precipice, seeing his wife's
    dying cancer in serenity
on the forest of burning Mahayana texts
Peter on the run from his soul
promising his lonely little son that he'd be home for
    the holidays
but he's stuck in the Himalayas of Nepal in the 1970s
knowing he wouldn't make it because of the damn fickle
Snow Leopard he had to lay marvelous snow-crusty eyes
    on the
spotted predator, walking all this way
in his sneakers.

The flu settles like a bastard son
as do the deceitful holidays
my mother finds the pilgrims clarity
in the St. Charles snow.

Big Jim's Lone Satellite

The Southeast Missouri sky
the addict's hunger
the gray tooth of streetlights
the dark dream.
Lost among the banjo of the Skull and Crossbones
 dancefloor
the conductor whistles his lonely polyamorous kazoo
dreaming of a love so big
(as his locomotive spins on)
he could shoot a shotgun at the sky and
not even hit a single solitary star.
He hums to the moon that winks
like a discredited politician
his heart so big it's painful.
(What more could it include?)
He thinks of the bartender, Red pulling guns on the
 robbers that pulled guns on her,
Red bleeding red on the shaggy carpet
the news vans circling
(no smash n grab salvation).
He thinks of all the bad intentions on the planet
(Trumps little fingers on the nuclear codes)
the anarchist's social war becomes
a war of the heart
like a squatter's barrel fire
behind a Tennessee roadhouse.

He summons Tinder looking for his big love fix,
swiftly puts it down for
reality. Setting love on fire.
It was the best of times
and the worst of society. A cop
car on fire, a jogger
running through the communal darkness of
Tower Grove Park at 11pm, the underage wine
the jogger remembers consuming
lust, the abandoned cut-off jeans
the fingers twirling the zipper
the goth poets and the lights
of the park rangers.
Desire like Isaiah's trumpet at midnight
cutting the tendons of the moon. The legendary
night, I swear someday
this will all be legend,
a drunk ecstasy
she was one breakdown away from abandoning him
   even at that point.
The head given by the muggy banks
of the Missouri River
tall grass on the asshole.
The old man he's become
the grumpiness
too many years of DJ Shadow and demons,
the muscles in the Epsom Salt soak,
he picks up Tinder again
looking for an angry fix.

Writing your way through a Jupiter moon of heartache
   and potential.
The joy of the blues,
the atheist's shelter
forgotten Youporn pictures
jealousy and redemption and
compassion. Oh, to teach teenagers.
A Jurassic heart swelling of worlds.
A solitary satellite shoots across
Big Jim's darkness.

Big Jim's Commute

The lit roman candle of the afternoon sparkling
  in bitterness
the streets are flooded with sunset
and cheap heroin
(love in the open sky
that huge pothole of the sun swallowing the trucks
  on Gustine street
swallowing the sky).
A risk,
a shock of death.
A run through the darkness in the supermarket
  light avoiding needles.
No boutique here, just the dark and the crusted mattress
  beneath the bridge
blankets sticking to it like a barnacle.
The madness of the day
ends with the commute
guiding me on the run through the neighborhood
and Big Jim his gas guzzler clutch sticking
on 55, getting off to Carondelet.

Big Jim Dreams Lost Dream of the Belle Missouri Bookstore

Big Jim dreams lost dreams of the Belle Missouri
 bookstore
or the rivers of Osage Missouri where
Big Jim squats by the banks of the Gasconade
in the valley, the ashen fall besides the wood
 paneled ranches.

A naked punk
pink-Mohawk
drifts lazily by
a tire covering his junk
nipples erect
Jim offers him
a river flowers
he declines or doesn't hear or
doesn't understand
and floats on.

Big Jim goes back to his river stare and contemplates
 the inexplicable Tom Waits poster
and explicable paperback biographies of Nancy Reagan
in the Old Belle Missouri Bookstore.

Big Jim Gets His Wisdom Teeth Yanked

Big Jim gets his wisdom teeth
yanked at the ripe young age of 35
spends the day in a minor opiate haze
listening to *Let It Bleed*
craves leftover burrito
settles for smoothie
it's mid-January the blood discharging itself
from the empty teeth. Teeth
like the pain of the year 2017
pain he hopes is rotting in a garbage pile
of a Crestwood Oral Surgeon's office
gone and soon to be forgotten.

New Year

All the bad handwriting the
bad food from age 20-22
the wonderful sex the
awkward crash of bodies into
each other. I think of
the concrete images of time passing
like honey into tea.
Foam cresting on the mouth of the Mississippi
the tension of our bitterness
of our pain and delight.
The cafe with the Samuel Johnson quotation on the wall
(not the one about the beast-man)
the one that talks of love and light.
Years of writing encased in journals rotting in the
  wet boxes of my basement
a regular sacrifice
odd sensations of the Missouri River of time.
Van Gogh's night cafe
where I sit not going mad,
sane and writing.

Ode to The Wasteland

Stetson you whom I saw watching the barges drift by
  the Mississippi at Jefferson Barracks park
that corpse, that expired love you planted last April, has
  it begun to bloom yet?
Is it lost beneath a deer-eaten snowbank?
It's the almighty playing games with your heart through
  an iPhone app and 21st century relationship theories
  and free wine at an open mic in Dutchtown.
It's too many burritos, swigs of whiskey after the gym
  that make you think about death
of the cow and how you used to be too kind to consume
  meat.
It's like the better you get how alcohol starts to feel like
  ethanol and you are reminded of the illness caused by
  moonshine and how you were dry for a year after that.
My nerves are bad tonight.
Speak to me
hold me
spoon me
speak to me about the bad wars of art school
about bearing witness through social work
about the abyss of open love
under freaky bar light
under blankets
text me a text about Eliot's genderqueer despair;
If only I could feel another man's back.

The thunder in South St. Louis erupts
lightning over criminal streets
and fresh snow by the park's pond side.
What has the thunder given us?
To give
to sympathize
to control
the love of fine art
and friends in low places.
Downward dog
veganism
sparkling water
and the barbed wire of the workhouse where I visit
 my old clients.
Distance running and
rail whiskey.
T.S. Eliot's black-jack dealer goatee.
Oh, to grow up by the Big River and leave forever.
To grow old and eerily, obliviously conservative
to find a church
to look into ten-year old headlights
on the locomotives of Webster Groves.

St. Louis On Fire

The twang of an inner city miracle
lost beneath an elm growing out of a dumpster.
I'd sit by the river, sip a bitter root and let the barges
drift towards the city
Rick smoking insatiable in my memory.

I once heard of a fight where one man pushed another
    into the river
he flailed and met his end.
There I'd bike along that dusty fall trail, find used needles
search for evidence, answers
men muttering about violence
the voice of streets I could barely know or comprehend.

I got lost among a woods of brick apartment buildings
    and corner shops selling hookah
a woods of brick buildings lawless rules and a landscape
shaggy with elms and sponsored community gardens
Nikes strung across telephone poles.

The city's on fire
there are warring factions
I watch the river move.

Sean Arnold is a poet, writer and visual artist residing in South Saint Louis, Missouri. He graduated from Webster University in 2015 with a degree in Creative Writing where he was poetry editor of the *Green Fuse* literary magazine and studied under David Clewell. Arnold is currently pursuing a Master's in Education from Webster University, and his day job is as a community support provider at a mental health agency. Previous published works include a four-part chap book series called *Soliloquy from a Freight Yard*, which was based around freight yard romanticisms and the glorious confusion of youth. Previous publications include *Big Bridge Magazine out of Berkley*, *The Green Fuse*, and *Crossing the Divide* (an anthology created by St. Louis' poet laureate Michael Castro to promote unity through poetry). Past music credits include providing spoken word for the bands Barely Free and Holy!Holy!Holy!. For the past three years he has run a reading series out of Foam Coffee and Beer on Cherokee St. entitled Sunday Summer Spoken Word series. Arnold is a lover of dusty trails, back-alleys, freight trains, running, good health and bourbon.

This project was made possible, in part, by generous support from the Osage Arts Community.

Osage Arts Community provides temporary time, space and support for the creation of new artistic works in a retreat format, serving creative people of all kinds — visual artists, composers, poets, fiction and nonfiction writers. Located on a 152-acre farm in an isolated rural mountainside setting in Central Missouri and bordered by ¾ of a mile of the Gasconade River, OAC provides residencies to those working alone, as well as welcoming collaborative teams, offering living space and workspace in a country environment to emerging and mid-career artists. For more information, visit us at www.oac.com

Osage Arts Community

www.ingramcontent.com/pod-product-compliance
Lightning Source LLC
Chambersburg PA
CBHW021451080526
44588CB00009B/795